LET'S TALK ABOUT...
BOYS

Copyright © 2021 by Emerald Rising, LLC

All rights reserved. No part of this publication may be reproduced or used in any manner without written permission of the author except for the use of quotations in a book review.

Table of Contents

Dedication: To My Girls 01
Let's Talk About...Boys Pledge 02
Preface: Did She Know? (A Letter to my Mommy) 03
Introduction: How Did I Get Here? 05

Section 1: ...The Men 08
Chapter 1: Why Doesn't He Want Me? 09
Chapter 2: Why Can't I Be? 15
Chapter 3: Why Did They Have to Go? 23

Section 2: ...My Body 33
Chapter 4: Why Am I Fat? 34
Chapter 5: What is Happening to My Body? 40

Section 3: ...Boys 46
Chapter 6: How Do I Get Him to Like Me? 47
Chapter 7: What's Affection? 57
Chapter 8: Why Am I Not Good Enough? 65

Section 4: ...The Talk 73
Chapter 9: Should I Know About This? 74
Chapter 10: Why Should I Wait? 79

Conclusion: How to Keep the Conversation Going? 89
Discussion Guide 90

To My Girls

This book is for the lonely girl who feels she has no one to talk to. This book is for the girl that thinks she can't fit in. This book is for the girl that has been abandoned and rejected. This book is for the girl who suffers from anxiety. This book is for the girl still trying to figure out who she is. This book is for the girl that wants to be loved.

This book is for the mother who lost her way. This book is for mothers that are still dealing with trauma. This book is for the mother that is overwhelmed by the demands of life. This book is for the mother that has a hard time communicating. This book is for mothers with daughters.

This book is for all the women that want to break cycles.

I pray girls will find comfort and safety by confiding in their mothers about any and everything. And I hope moms are able to set aside time to sit their daughters down to say, Let's Talk About...Boys.

Let's Talk About...Boys Pledge

On this day and forevermore, We pledge to be open, honest and accepting to one another. As we sit down in conversation, I will keep my heart clear, and my thoughts free of judgment. We have created a safe space for our interactions to be comfortable and secure. Anger is off the table, and there is no need to be right or wrong. We will honor each other in understanding, peace, and love.

_____ _____

Signature   Date

_____ _____

Signature   Date

Did She Know?

(A Letter to my Mommy)

As kids, we think our parents are so old, just because they are our parents. In the first grade, while discussing my mother's age, 28, with a classmate, I felt that we were worlds apart. As an adult now, I see how my perception was totally off. My mother and I are only 22 years apart. She was pregnant at the age of 21. 21, the year that marks full legalization, and the start of adulthood. When I think about myself at the age of 21, thoughts of me drinking, partying, and thinking only about myself come to mind. 21 is the age to explore oneself, start careers, and have fun with minimum responsibilities, but for my mom, she was prepping for her most immense responsibility to date, with no how-to manual for her preparation.

I can imagine she felt some guilt and shame, knowing she disappointed her parents by having a baby out of wedlock. I can assume she underwent a moment of fear and worry, knowing that she would possibly have to move out of her parents' home and would have to raise a baby alone. I cannot fathom the helplessness she endured when her baby girl took control of her body with severe morning sickness, prompting a hospitalization and an alarming weight loss.

Having me at the age of 22, she provided the best life that she could; a roof over my head, clothes, food, and a two-parent household by marrying my stepfather. I appreciate it all. In my 30's, I still don't have it all together, but at my age, 33, she was navigating a marriage, raising two girls, and processing grief. I never saw my mother break; I never knew the times she struggled, where she cried and dropped to her knees to pray. She always displayed strength. I attempted to mirror her, never trying to break. Cry? My mom didn't, so why would I? We are strong; we pray and move on. I wonder if she knew I needed to see her vulnerability, I wonder if she saw my struggles, and I wonder if she was just too afraid to bring them to the forefront because it would ultimately break her heart.

My Mommy and I grew up under two different circumstances. She lived with her biological father in the home. I did not. Speaking to her the day I decided to cut off communication with my father, she confirmed our differences. She told me that she could not speak to my decision because she has not experienced the abandonment and rejection I faced. At that moment, I knew she knew my heart and the brokenness of it but did not know what to do to heal it. I can't say my life would have been any different if my mom and I had a closer relationship, if she became my first best friend. I pray our missed communications and missed opportunities to get to know each other encourage all generations to build better connections within the home. More importantly, I want my Mommy to know that her unconditional love was and is felt, even if it was not always spoken. I want her to find comfort in knowing that she did nothing wrong in raising me. My journey had to be my journey for a higher purpose. For that, I'm thankful.

How Did I Get Here?

To stop anything catastrophic from happening, preventative measures must be in place to help alleviate damage. Preparing early for significant events can make a tremendous difference in the outcome and impact of the matter. Taking the initiative needed to slow unwarranted events and situations is a critical concept to understand. COVID-19 was going to happen. It was inevitable, but it could have been controlled, therefore having a little less impact, especially in the United States. Instead, the people in higher positions in the country waited until the virus was in full force, making it hard to control, and giving rise to inadequate equipment, overcrowded hospitals, overworked essential workers, and way too many deaths. Overall, leaving the country exhausted, riddled with anxiety, and full of anger.

Most traumas and situations that we face could have been prevented, or unavoidable situations could have had less of a negative impact on our future if appropriately managed. Poor management of cycles, whether trauma, negative mindsets, or the lack of connections, were reasons why I did not have proper, informative, and challenging conversations with the adults in my life as an adolescent.

Not hearing I was beautiful, being forced to change what I looked like because of my larger stature, not hearing I love you, or a sorry when I felt hurt, all played a part in my teenage years and womanhood development.

To become a woman dedicated to the growth journey, you must have an acceptance and appreciation for the adults in your life. You learn that they have their issues and things to deal with daily outside of raising children. Sometimes those issues take precedence over having those crucial conversations and moments with their children. A conscious effort of affirming their children can be a slip of the mind, or may not seem as important as keeping food and the lights on in the house. Providing financial stability is the focus, and the mental and emotional strength of the child becomes an afterthought.

Then there is the contention of adult superior, child inferior mentality. "What I say is right," "do what I say, not what I do," "I'm not one of your little friends" are some of the critical phrases heard within the household. When adults present themselves in this manner to their developing child, they come off as intimidating, making it uncomfortable for your child to ask questions, be comfortable with expressing themselves, and sharing their inner thoughts and struggles.

What does that child do? Where does she get her advice? Does she go talk to her friend who is the same age, with a child's mentality, who gets all their "grown-up" information from the internet or television? The answer is yes, and that results in the blind leading the blind. Truth, a child needs to be mentally nurtured, shaped to take on society's ugliness, and given compassion and grace to figure out how to navigate through this world.

You are probably wondering what gives me the right to write this book? Let me tell you. I was one of those girls that had to figure out things by myself. In my process of growing up, can you guess the number one thing that piqued my interest? BOYS! Boys were always on my mind. Some would say I was fast, hot in the pants, or too grown acting. Instead of someone talking to me about my newfound interest, my feelings, and why I was so intrigued by the male species, I felt like my feelings were wrong, unacceptable, and brought about shame and confusion.

There was no deeper thought as to why this girl was boy-crazy at the age of 8. If it did occur to them, no one talked to me about it or mentioned it. Life kept pushing, and I made my own decisions with my limited understanding. These decisions ultimately came with a price - the price of self. I wish my mom and the other adults around me would have known that my self-esteem, self-worth, and self-awareness were linked to their influence, and I needed them emotionally while growing up.

I will not say I am not grateful for my journey, but Lord, it was a lot. I am now here with my story and insight on how a strong sense of self-esteem in teenage years and young adulthood can contribute to fewer traumas, healthy friendships, and courtships, but more importantly, a healthy relationship with self. I hope that this book brings teen daughters and their mothers together. Opening the dialogue to help, motivate, and encourage young women to take control of their own lives, walk in their confidence, and love in the proper way. Let's Talk About...Boys.

...The Men

Why Doesn't He Want Me?

I always felt my body was way mature for my age; men telling me I had child-bearing hips and following me around the neighborhood. However, my mentality was way more mature than the derriere I possessed. I grew up way before I should, not because I had to help support my family or take care of younger siblings, but because I was left to deal with my emotions and internal issues alone. I was left to figure out one major thing: how a man can have a baby but does the bare minimum to be in the baby's life.

I saw my father on occasions. Specifically, I remember him showing up for Christmas, me running down the hall and jumping in his arms and hugging my older brother. He would pick me up to go to his sister's house, my aunt, for Christmas dinner. This event always made me happy, complete even. The excitement of seeing my older cousin, who I happen to be named after and looked up to, was immeasurable. I would also see my grandmother, who at the time could not walk or talk due to her having Multiple Sclerosis, but being in her presence was a gift in itself.

I was elated to be with my daddy and family once a year. The few hours we had were just enough. Until it wasn't. The visits stopped, and I did not see my family all together again. The last interaction I had was visiting my aunt and cousin, where I received the movie Matilda. It was my favorite gift and the last gift I would ever get from that side of the family. I was 8 or 9 at the time.

The details of the years where my dad would show up, to the time he completely stopped is a blur. There is no significance. Only seeing him once or twice a year left no memories stamped into my hippocampus. What was significant is that over the years, I became angry, hurt, and bitter. I could not understand what happened as to why I was no longer wanted in the life of the man who created me. What had I done wrong? Why doesn't he love me?

My heart was filled with resentment by his disappearance, missed phone calls, and deserted holidays. When I was nine years old, I had grown so annoyed with my dad that the disappointment slowly turned to hate. He excitedly called me one day. He wanted to tell me that I had a new baby brother. A typical reaction would have been to be excited; a new brother that I can play with, hold, tease, but I knew, in reality, I would not have this kind of relationship with my baby brother. Sadly, my assumption was accurate. I would not meet my brother until the age of 17.

I listened to the news angrily for two reasons. I wouldn't have a bond with this new precious baby boy, and my thought was, how the hell is this man raising another kid and can't even call me. I must have been agitated because apparently, I did not hang up the phone at the end of the conversation. I went off, and my dad heard it. Instead of calling back and figuring out why I was angry or talking about it, he decided to take in the words I expressed and hold it against me.

This kind of pain associated with rejection and abandonment becomes internalized. My dad not being around felt as though his actions were the effect of something I did. I felt empty, ashamed, and afraid that my father would never love me. If he deems me unworthy of calling and showing love, will anyone else see me worthy? These thoughts and feelings created a hole in my heart that I had to mend on my own.

I learned to protect myself, and that was not the best thing to do. I had no answers. I could not understand my feelings and behaviors linked to this rejection and abandonment. When I was supposed to be shaped by my parental influences to build healthy self-esteem and self-worth, I was left with disappointment and extreme confusion. I had no insight that the longing feeling for that unconditional love you can only get from a daddy would be associated with me doing anything to gain boys' approval and attention to feel something.

The comfort from a daddy is something every girl needs and longs for. He should be her protector, her first love, and a model for what type of boys she should bring home. When her heart is broken, Daddy should nurture and mend the broken pieces. However, when a father is absent from a daughter's life, she is left with half of the heart missing. I like to believe that a child's heart is made of two beats; one from mom and one from dad, intertwined to make a really dope beat. My heartbeat had no kick drum or bass. When you don't feel your dad's love, your heartbeat lacks significant components and leaves your heart defective. For me, my void left me to seek attention from boys. I was always looking to feel complete and whole. My self-conscious mind processed this as my dad is a boy, so any boy can fill the hole in my heart.

Though I couldn't physically feel pain, it was ingrained inside of me. I felt lost and was always searching for someone who would take these thoughts away and make me feel happy. I became boy-crazy. I was the aggressor. I made boys like or tried to make them like me. I would call all the time, ride my bike around their houses to be seen. The crusade to not feel broken led me to desperation, embarrassment, and loneliness. I did not know, and no one explained that chasing boys would not make me feel loved. No one told me that what I needed from my father could only come from my father.

I wish my dad would have known that as well, but it appeared it was not his concern. As a child, this emptiness was not my responsibility and was definitely not the responsibility of the boys I encountered. Imagine the energy I put into the atmosphere and what the guys were thinking and feeling from my aggressiveness. I am sure I made them uncomfortable amid my uncomfortableness. These patterns stayed with me for over 20 years, up until my last relationship at the age of 29.

Not hearing affirmations or being assured of my worthiness, I took it upon myself to prove it to myself. When you have to prove something, you go to great lengths to receive validation. My confidence was remarkable, but for all the wrong reasons. I was willing to get what I needed, which meant going beyond the parameters of my age mentality. I became comfortable with being uncomfortable; from kissing boys in front of all my friends, to hiding behind buildings showing and seeing body parts. The most dangerous thing is that I offered before even being asked. I wanted to assure myself and others that someone was going to like what I was offering and ultimately love me.

Let's Talk About It

Reflect on these questions to process the chapter's topics to help navigate an open and honest conversation. Some of these topics may be uncomfortable, but that's okay. To have the conversation is much needed and will help build a healthier and closer relationship. As the girls answers the questions, ladies reflect on your childhood and adolescence to be empathetic and share experiences and feelings you felt or feel as it relates to the topics within the chapter.

♦ Does this chapter bring up a topic that you would like to discuss?

♦ How can you relate to this chapter?

♦ Does it trigger a memory?

♦ What is the memory?

♦ What emotions surfaced while reading this chapter?

♦ Why do you think these emotions came to surface?

_____

_____

_____

_____

_____

_____

Why Can't I Be?

(Walking on Eggshells)

As a child, I believe I had a direct personality, saying what came to mind and freely expressing my wants. Most children do. There are no boundaries because they have not learned the societal norm codes. If a kid feels like something is ugly or a person looks different, they bring attention to it with no filter or remorse. Children are the most honest individuals. The adults in their lives begin to filter their minds and teach them what is appropriate to say. In society, we try hard not to make others feel uncomfortable with our actions. We are taught to be caring individuals, and to be nice to everyone, treating them with dignity and respect. It is not outside of the norm for parents to correct their children when they don't honor the feelings of others. However, when parents take away a child's freedom from their personal feelings, thoughts, moods, and creativity, it stirs up confusion, conflict, and discouragement on the kid's behalf.

At a young age, there is a sense of self-freedom that is so beautiful. The risks kids take, the unsheltered imagination, and their inquisitive minds are to be cherished. On the contrary, adults have been through many experiences that have altered their innocence. Somehow, they subconsciously bring the burden of their lives to their children, slowly but surely stripping the kid's freedoms and journey of self-discovery.

Everyone has bad days where you are more irritable, and any and everything bothers you to the core. A person looks at you funny, and you are ready to go off type of days. At home, some parents don't know how to separate the world from their children. A child could be their typical goofy self, being free, laughing, exploring, and doing the things they enjoy. Still, just because the parent is having a bad day, they automatically start yelling at the kid, halting their fun.

The child may not be doing anything harmful or wrong, but because the parent is tired or angry, they ultimately make the kid suffer with them. Their freedom and fun are now associated with yelling and being told no. It makes them feel that what they are doing, how they express themselves, or what they enjoy is wrong. What seems minor can be mentally and emotionally damaging to the child.

Around the age of 6 or 7, my family took a trip to Marion, Alabama. I am assuming it was a family reunion. One day on our mini-vacation, some of the family went swimming. I cannot speak to all the details, it was almost 30 years ago, but my stepsister was told not to go into a particular section in the pool. The way she was told made things uneasy for me, and even at a young age, I had to make the situation light again. My stepfather presented his concern in a more aggressive than caring tone. It made me embarrassed for my sister and my mom.

When we got back from the pool, I jokingly said something about my sister not being able to go to the deep end because she would have drowned. It wasn't a funny joke. I was 7 I didn't have my wits at the time. It was also not a false claim, but somehow, it offended my stepfather. You would have thought I was a grown man cursing him out by his reaction towards me. I'm not sure if something else went down that day, but when we got back to our hotel, he came at me, a kid.

It scared me. I have never seen my stepfather in this light. He was nothing but friendly and fun when it involved me. I was not prepared for his words, his tone, his anger. I knew what he was doing was wrong, because my mother jumped to my defensive swiftly. After going back and forth, a scuffle broke out. I saw my mom on the floor, pinned to the corner, tussling and hitting her way free. I have never witnessed anything like this in my 7 years of life. It was traumatizing, to say the least. I have never seen my mom so angry, so fearless, and yet so fragile. I have never seen my stepfather so angry, so mean. If I would have never said anything, then this disaster of an altercation would have never happened. It was all my fault. I felt guilt and uneasiness from that day.

Apologies were had, we moved on as a family, and majority of our days were good, but to say I was 100% relaxed at home is farfetched. Throughout the years as more incidents occurred, the more I learned to pretend that everything was okay even though I had to walk on eggshells to make sure I didn't step on the grenade living in my home. At times it felt like I lived with a ticking time bomb, and it was only a matter of time before it would be a grand gesture of anger within the four walls of our home. No specific time or special day was exempt from the wrath.

Being around other family members became stressful for me. If someone said something that my stepdad did not like, his disdain was felt. His volatile actions weren't as scary as I got older, but they were more embarrassing and draining and, at times, heartbreaking. When my stepfather came into my life, he was literally my best friend. He played with me all the time and made everything fun. It was a great situation for me, especially not seeing my dad often. My stepfather is an incredible person. I can't take that away from him. He is caring and passionate, but everyone has less desirable character traits, and anger was one of his.

I could not trust him and kept my guard up around him. Being a teenager going through my phase of teenager woes was the most difficult time living with him. Not to mention High School brought about another set of issues, because you know, boys. He was not affectionate nor did he show a sensitive side. Being goofy was his way to do things.

There was a time that I was not in the mood; having a mood swing or something. I'm not sure what was exactly wrong, but I couldn't deal that day. I told my stepdad to leave me alone - my issue was not towards him, but he took it personally. He left me alone. He ignored me for days. I was heartbroken and felt another form of rejection. Our relationship would never be the same in my eyes.

Discipline looked different for me within the household. As far as my mom, she may have brought out the belt, yelled a little, or taken away my phone or something. My stepdad, he destroyed things—holes in the walls, busted TV, and broken lamps. In the summer going into my senior year, my momma decided to update my room to more of a sophisticated look compared to my Mickey Mouse decor. During her interior design process, I was placed in the basement to stay. The update took a while. There was new paint, an updated dresser and bookshelf, and a new bed. She went all out. I can admit I liked living in the basement during the renovation, and I took an extra day or two to move back to my room. I slowly started moving back into my room. When my stepdad came home one day after work, he saw I was not completely moved back into my room, and he flipped. He started destroying my newly remodeled bedroom. Nothing warrants your belongings being continuously destroyed. He was dealing with personal things; had it been work that day, maybe, but no one in the home should have witnessed and felt his rage. That was the last straw for me emotionally. I knew that I never wanted to stay at that house, but I had nowhere to go. I just had to go on with my days pretending everything was great, something we did as a family.

I knew nothing about going to college out of state, members of my family never lived outside of St. Louis or attended school away. But I knew that I had to get away from the city and needed a break from my family. When it was my opportunity to leave, I went far enough away that I could only see my family on holidays, but close enough that it would not take days to travel home. I hated leaving my mom, but I just wanted to feel safe and at peace without having to worry about the next explosion. As a girl with daddy issues, the most painful thing is that I had to carry the weight of another man, not considering my feelings and heart safety.

The worse factor is that being around this type of behavior becomes embedded in your habits. The yelling, hitting, quick to anger, all became of me. To add insult to injury, I attracted people that were like my stepfather. Even though I did not grow up in a comfortable and emotionally healthy situation, my stepfather's behaviors exhibited within others were familiar and, in a sense, expected. I was drawn to the people that were like the person I was running from. They say a girl will date and marry someone like her father, and everyone I dated either reflected my biological father or stepfather. I had the worst of both worlds.

Let's Talk About It

- Does this chapter bring up a topic that you would like to discuss?
- How can you relate to this chapter?
- Does it trigger a memory?
- What is the memory?
- What emotions surfaced while reading this chapter?
- Why do you think these emotions came to surface?

_____

_____

_____

_____

_____

_____

_____

_____

_____

_____

_____

_____

Why Did They Have to Go?

I don't really understand how or exactly when I got to the state of intense worry. When I reflect on my childhood, I did not anxiously wait for bad things to happen. I was pretty confident in my abilities and did things I wanted without thinking about how others viewed me. If bad things were to happen, my bounce-back was quick, and I did not associate that incident with unforeseeable situations in my future. I had times where peers treated me differently because of my weight, but for the most part, I marched to the beat of my own drum, without worries. I often wonder if I masked things at a young age, knowing that life was full of disappointments, and I just taught myself to smile anyway and forget about the less desirable situations.

My relationship with my dad and my adjustment to having a stepfather should have warranted me to seek a therapist. However, growing up in a black family - a black family within the church - therapy was never an option. My mental health and anxiety became a question when death hit me. The grief forever changed me, making me face all my unresolved emotions.

Most girls are daddy's girls, but me, I was a Grandpa's girl. The love that I had for Monsieur, my nickname I gave him after taking a French summer course, ran deep. He was always there for me. Our forever bond started when he would hold me as an infant during my early morning wake-ups. He would be walking in the door from his night shift as my mom was getting ready for work. My mom and I stayed with my grandparents for the first six years of my life. With the absence of my father, my Grandpa took the plate.

I was extremely attached to him. My mom told me that one day while he was moving his clothes from the upstairs closet to his closet downstairs, she and my aunt jokingly told me he was moving out. I distraughtly yelled, "Grandpa, where the hell are you going?!" I was 2 or 3 years old at the time. That was my first curse word.

My Grandpa was the kindest and the gentlest being. He was genuinely nice to everyone, and you could feel his love without him saying a word. He did not talk too much, but when he did, everyone was drawn to listen. The car rides are what I remember the most. He would pick me up from the bus stop during my elementary and middle school years. We would listen to Gospel and Country music, depending on the day, but hearing him sing would bring me so much comfort.

I knew he would always be there for me, until the day I saw my Grandpa bent over in pain. The panic in my family's face terrified me. The first time I had extreme fear and no control. I felt that if anything were to happen to my Grandpa, I could not live. Life wouldn't make sense. It turns out that the health scare was just kidney stones. I had a little bit of relief, but seeing my Grandpa in such a weak state put me on guard.

The next health scare was when he had a staring spell on the airplane coming from Miami. He drew blank and did not move or respond. He went straight to the hospital after getting off the plane and had to stay overnight. I tried my hardest to avoid visiting him. I couldn't see him vulnerable and sick. When I got to the hospital, he reassured me that he was and would be okay. It was a seizure he had. Since that day, in my eyes, he was never the same. I was always afraid and worried that something was going to happen to him at any time.

As I grew older and he grew older, so did my fear. I loved my Grandpa so much, but I would be more anxious than comfortable around him after he got sick. I could not wrap my head around the thought of him not being as strong and healthy as I once knew he was. People not knowing him personally would not have guessed he had previous medical issues. He was still active, worked an overnight job, and drove across the states to drop me off and pick me up from college. Still, there was a dark cloud that followed me with the worry of something happening to him. I could not mentally handle it.

Until I had to handle it.

Being busy in college, sometimes you don't always call home every day. College life is demanding. I don't think I talked to my Grandpa for a week or two. He had come down to drop me off at college in August, and that time was a little different for me. He seemed so much more vulnerable.

One night in September, I had the most disturbing dream. I was at a funeral of what I believed to be one of my uncle's, but it was my Grandpa when I looked in the casket. I woke up immediately in a panic. I waited an hour or two before calling home to check on him. When I called, he was at work, and my grandma told me that he was doing okay. Life went on for another week. A week from the night I had the dream, my world was turned upside down. Around 9pm, my roommate and I made a run to Sonic. My mom had called me every day and every night, but that night she did not. I called her; she did not answer. I tried my Godmother; it was her birthday, so maybe my mom was with her. She did not answer. I called my grandparents' home. They did not answer. I called my aunt's house. She did not answer. I called my cousins; they did not answer.

I began to get sick to my stomach. I had no clue what was going on, but something was not right. I went back to my dorm, and my stomach was in knots. I went to the restroom, and while I was in there, I heard a voice say, "I am going to be okay." I knew it was my Grandpa and that everything was going to be okay. As I exited the restroom, my cousin was there. She told me my Grandpa passed away. I did not believe her. My older cousin, who was on the phone, confirmed his death. I lost it.

My biggest nightmare had come true. It was an indescribable feeling. I want to believe I handled everything well; I had my moments that I would breakdown, but then a sense of peace would suddenly come over me. I did not die with my Grandpa, but a piece of my heart died that day. It is comforting during the funeral process when there are so many people around. It is easy to carry on and even laugh. The family gathering temporarily distracts you from the heartache and devastation. A week after the arrangements, I headed back to school, alone, with a new frame of mind.

Returning to school was a blur, and I am not sure how I made it through the day, but I did. I tried to act as normal as possible, but I don't think I was ever the same. However, through this time, I did not cry. I did not grieve. I felt numb. There was no one to talk to, so I kept my feelings in, smiling and appearing to be normal. My family and I did not talk about my Grandpa's death. In their defense, we were all hit with sudden death. My Grandpa was the rock of the family. I knew everyone grieved how they saw fit. The advantage of their grief was that they had each other. They saw one another weekly, ate Sunday dinner together, and had the comfort of knowing family was there, even if they did not express their feelings. I did not. I was alone to deal with something I had never experienced before, something traumatic.

I had no control over my grandfather's death, but from that day, I subconsciously tried to control everything because of the dread of something horrible happening again. I worried about others constantly and about the older people in my family. If someone was sick, I feared that at any time, they were going to die. The underlying thought was that if I prepared myself for awful situations to happen, then I would not be so affected by them. That was no way to live.

My every waking day wasn't in gloom, and as the days and months went by, I got back to a routine. I excelled in school, joined a professional fraternity, Sigma Tau Epsilon, and had a relatively good social life. Dealing with death is something you will never get over but something you learn to live with.

I was doing okay, but then my biggest fear came true again, and I could never have prepared for the blow that was coming upon my life. During Thanksgiving Break of my Junior year, one year and two months after my grandfather passed, I was faced with another tragic loss.

Partying on Thanksgiving nights after spending time with your family was the thing to do. I was excited this particular Thanksgiving because my dear friend was going to be at the same party. Let me provide a little background information. This guy cared for me immensely; he was funny, and we had a tight bond. I had no clue who he was in High School until one of my bandmates told me he wanted to talk to me. I was not impressed. One day while in band class, this guy came from his class to have a conversation with me. I was immediately embarrassed. I wouldn't say I liked the attention, and this gesture made it seem like everyone was looking at me. I am quite sure no one cared. We exchanged numbers, but I was not interested.

As we talked on the phone, almost every day, a true friendship formed. He wanted to be my boyfriend, but I did not see him in that way. Someone finally chose me, and I rejected them. Well, control was the issue. I wanted my knight in shining armor to be someone I wanted, who I was attracted to, someone to look, in my eyes, perfect. My dear friend did not fit that criteria, but I loved him.

I loved hanging with him, but my need for control and low self-esteem did not let me let go of trivial things. He still pursued me, and in his pursuit, we became closer until our sophomore year in college. I am not sure what all transpired, but we stopped talking. I can admit, my actions stemmed from him having a girlfriend, and I was not number one on his list anymore.

Back to Thanksgiving break: I called him when I got into the city the day before to see if he was home. We had small formalities, and just like that, we were back to normal. The night of the party I was so excited to see him, I jumped in his arms in front of everyone. I never felt that much joy. The last time I jumped into anyone's arms was my father's the last Christmas he would show up. That is how special he was to me. We stepped away from the party to talk. He looked at me with admiration. The feeling was different - a good different. I was ready to be with him.

After leaving the party, we talked on the phone from leaving the venue to a food stop at White Castle, to home. I got off the phone with him to get in the house safely and talk to my mom briefly. I called him back, he did not answer but texted, saying he would call me in a few minutes. He never did. He just continued to text. The texts were strange, like an ending in a sense. I kept telling him to call me, but he continued to text. "You will always be my Limpy, and I will always be your Fat Azz." That was the last text I got from him.

The next day, printing coupons to go Black Friday shopping, my friend that I was going shopping with called me. She asked if I talked to a friend of ours, which was a weird question. Why would I need to speak to them? I immediately had that gut feeling something was wrong, and for some reason, I knew it was about my Fat Azz.

I called his phone immediately. His father answered, and he told me that he was gone. I did not ask for details, and still, to this day, I don't know what happened. I know I was the last person that he talked to. My first real admirer, a true friend, was now gone out of my life so suddenly, at the mere age of 20 years old, and there was nothing I could do about it.

Another trauma that I was left to figure out and grieve alone. My mom thought it was best I didn't go to the funeral, I'm sure, to protect me from seeing him lying in the casket, but I needed that closure. I dreamed almost every night of the funeral, and what he looked like at peace, but it still did not heal my wounded heart and ease the anxiety. Experiencing someone my age die, so suddenly, my fear changed from worrying about an older family member dying, to I am going to die, or my friends will die at any moment. The thoughts stayed in my head, repeatedly.

Due to the sadness, the numbness, I laid in my bed mostly. I did not want to be around anyone. By my last year of college, I appeared to be okay, but I was completely withdrawn. No one noticed, but I felt alone, and my anxiety grew. The trauma of two deaths and the constant worry intensified my fear of rejection and abandonment from childhood. My soul was heavy and my mind jumbled and foggy. Yet, I kept everything to myself. At this time in my life, I became accustomed to not discussing my feelings and the undesirable events in my life. I just continued to press forward while suppressing everything. The suppression stunted my emotional growth and was a hit to my mental health. I lived in fear for years, not enjoying the pleasures of my 20's but just existing to prevent turmoil.

Let's Talk About It

- Does this chapter bring up a topic that you would like to discuss?
- How can you relate to this chapter?
- Does it trigger a memory?
- What is the memory?
- What emotions surfaced while reading this chapter?
- Why do you think these emotions came to surface?

_____

_____

_____

_____

_____

_____

_____

_____

_____

_____

_____

_____

_____

...My Body

Why Am I Fat?

My body has always been a thing for as long as I can remember. My belly became rounded at the age of seven or eight, and my face started filling out. I used to love to eat. At times eating became a competition between my stepfather and me. You can say it was our bonding time. It only became an issue when I became the chubby one in the family. My mom, grandma, aunts, and cousin were all under a size 8. My mom being a size zero, did not know what to do with me, her chubby child, that at the age of 12, weighed more than 60lbs over her small frame.

The 90's style is one of my favorite fashion eras; the crop tops, and the plaid miniskirts with matching vests or blazers. I watched the movie Clueless every Friday to get my fashion fix. I wanted to be and dress exactly like Cher. It was almost impossible for a girl with a stomach, thighs, and butt to find replicas of these adorable outfits in my size. I like to think my sense of style was created because I was always left to improvise my look to get close to the fashion trends throughout my teenage years.

My weight was not an issue for me until going to public school in the 3rd grade. I became the topic of jokes because I was new and fat. I was ignored and felt isolated from the other girls in my class. It is funny how children flock to one particular kid in their social circles, putting them on a pedestal and following their every move. When one of the popular girls in my class told all the other girls not to be my friend, they did it. The third grade was an unpleasant time for me and made me face the reality that the way you look is a determining factor in the way people treat you, which is absolutely ridiculous.

It was one thing to endure the cruelty of kids laughing and not wanting to be your friend because of a few extra pounds, but when your grandma gives you girdles to wear while you sleep to shrink your stomach, the shame surfaces. You may ask what a girdle is. Today it would be considered a body shaper but not as cool. In the '90s, it appeared to be a long bra; some had floral stitching prints, and some were plain that hooked in the front and covered the entire stomach. Needless to say, girdles were for grandmothers only.

At 8, this body armor did not quite work for my body type. You see, you needed boobs to fill out the cups, and even though I had little mosquito bites because of my weight, it still left tons of fabric in the chest area. I could either stuff my bra or cut the chest part out. I chose the latter, but it still looked a mess.

On top of the uncomfortableness of my granny girdles, I had to do Tae Bo, a kickboxing workout tape, with my mom's friends every Saturday. I wouldn't say I liked it. On my Saturdays I wanted to play, watch cartoons. I did not want to double up on the standing stomach crunches with women in their 30's. It was embarrassing and made me feel even more ashamed. I felt like I was being punished because of the way I looked. Being forced to try and change your body to fit societal norms at such a young age does something to you, your self-esteem. To this day, I hate exercising. The thought of having people hold me accountable for exercising turns me off, and I rebel.

The rebellion stems from not meeting the expectation of losing weight when I was younger. All my family's efforts to make me a desirable weight or reach the goal of wearing outfits with my belly showing still did not change the fact that I was a bigger girl. If only the world were more accepting of plumper individuals as they are now, I would not have to feel ashamed of how I looked in my own home.

I can admit that my stomach is still an insecurity of mine, and though I dress the way I want, belly out and all, I am still uncomfortable to wear outfits around my family in fear they will say something about my weight. As I came into my teen years, I did not show my insecurities on the forefront. I was still cute, but as my weight fluctuated back and forth and brought to my attention often either by my mom, the stores not having my size, or not being looked at by the opposite sex, I internally felt less than. People noticed me because of my weight, but I felt invisible at the same time. Regardless of how I wanted to be happy, I had outside sources that made me think that my body was wrong, gross, and not enough. My self-identity became more about my physical appearance than who I was as a person. When judgment comes from others before they get to know you, it hurts, but it is more damaging when your family tries to change your appearance.

As an adult, I now know my family loved me and did not intentionally want to hurt me. I will assume they saw how cruel the world is and thought that losing weight would help me dodge the venom spewed from society. I appreciate their protection. However, I needed to learn how to love myself - every part of it. I should have known that my body is not flawed but beautiful, regardless of whether it did not look like my peers. Instead, I doubted myself often and was at constant war with myself when I looked in the mirror. I needed kindness and compassion from the people I saw every day to build my confidence and realize my self-worth.

Affirmations should start in the home. Being a plus size girl and having the thoughts of being undesirable, I overcompensated in interacting with others. I adopted the mindsight that I had to prove myself worthy instead of just knowing I was worthy. Whether it is a little extra weight or the color of the skin, the overdeveloped or the underdeveloped, as a teen girl, the topic of their bodies and image is a susceptible subject.

Going through the hormonal and physical changes is enough to already deal with. Adding the pressures of societal beauty standards makes it even harder for self-acceptance. Body image should not be a big deal, but our culture has made it the focus of our existence. Girls need to be continuously affirmed, treated like princesses, and realize that they are beautiful. No matter what!

Let's Talk About It

- Does this chapter bring up a topic that you would like to discuss?
- How can you relate to this chapter?
- Does it trigger a memory?
- What is the memory?
- What emotions surfaced while reading this chapter?
- Why do you think these emotions came to surface?

_____

_____

_____

_____

_____

_____

_____

_____

_____

_____

_____

_____

What is Happening to My Body?

Have you ever noticed toddlers ask a lot of questions as they grow? What's that? What's this? Especially when it comes to the body. They are intrigued by what is a part of their body and what is different when they look at others, whether it be their siblings or parents. The adults answer their questions, labeling the body parts and expanding their knowledge as they grow. It is funny the same toddlers become pre-teens, and no one wants to talk to them about the changes that their body is about to experience.

It's time...to have...the talk. Watching television shows growing up, "the talk" was the dreaded conversation parents had to have with their teens uncomfortably, and the teens had to sit through it awkwardly. Although I felt that I would be embarrassed to have that conversation with my mom, grandma, or aunts, the talk never came. I had an older sister, so I vaguely knew about getting a menstrual cycle, but I saw firsthand what getting a period look liked by my fourth-grade classmates. They talked about it as if it was a badge of honor and would purposely put their used bloody pads on the bathroom floor. I guess to make us non-period having girls jealous.

It was also in the fourth-grade that the nurse came into our classrooms. The boys and girls were separated between all the fourth-grade classes. We had the growth presentation about what our bodies would be going through for the years to come.

It wasn't until middle school that we went deeper. There were presentations about how to put on condoms, and pictures of STDs. I still have a vivid image in my head. Worst of all, we saw the actual birth of a child. To this day, I dread childbirth. While I have been scarred and scared from the goriness of genital warts and the baby's head crowning, the nurses did not tell us everything we needed to know.

The raging hormones that cause a snippiness in your tone and a roll in your eyes, your uterus tied in knots, the adding of 5lbs of bloat making you look three months pregnant, and worst of all, feeling plain ole ugly.

I remember getting my cycle when I was 12 years old. I had no symptoms that it was coming, or I just didn't know. Of course, I wasn't expecting it. When I first saw Susan - that's what I named her - I was excited, but at the same time, I was so embarrassed. I did not know what to do with this sudden change, and I knew I was not prepared for the responsibility that came with it. Maxi pads were hidden in the bedroom closet at my grandma's house, in a bag, as if they were secret and not to be seen. Or is that what I made up in my head? With that thought in mind, it made it hard for me to tell my mom. I did not tell anyone right away. I just went to the hidden bag and got me a pad.

I got my period the day before my Godmother's wedding. I remember being extra emotional, crying. Love is such a beautiful thing and can make anyone cry because of the joy it brings, but I know my emotions were tied to Susan as well. I carried the feeling of embarrassment the entire day. There was this fear that everyone could tell I was now a woman, and I constantly worried that I would leak, and people would be able to see what was new with me. The biggest issue was I couldn't quite understand what was happening to my body, and making it worse, I felt that I had no one to share these thoughts with, even though Susan was a once a month thing. It was no surprise that no one noticed or did not realize that I did not have my period for another year after my initial period. I knew this was not normal.

I wore panty liners, taking them from my mom's closet, for an entire year, just waiting for something that was supposed to show up every month. I was stood up by my own period. Missing periods for months would become the norm for me, but I would later find out that it was not the norm for others. It wasn't until 17 years later that I would be diagnosed with Polycystic Ovary Syndrome.

My unpredictable menstrual cycle made me feel self-conscious. I always thought someone could tell if I was on my period. It brought shame to having a period. I was also not prepared for the growth of my breasts. I no longer had buds because of my chubbiness, but full breast that came along with womanhood. Having breasts in addition to my big butt, I felt that I was always being stared at. Even though that was not the case.

The stigma of having a period was associated with something nasty and not looked at as a beautiful rite of passage into womanhood. Because of this, it made me feel weird, and I wanted to hide. It ultimately caused me not to look at my body, not appreciate it, and not notice the signs when something was wrong. I did not learn about my body.

The talk can be extremely uncomfortable, especially since older generations did not have that talk, and some are still uneasy with the things that are going on with their bodies. I get it. It's a private matter. But letting your daughter know that every woman goes through this is a necessary experience and can make them feel more excited about learning about their body. As an adult woman with PCOS, I have become cautious with learning everything about my body, paying attention to my symptoms, hormone changes, and even mood swings. My awareness gives me time and the freedom to embrace my monthly changes and gives me warning signs if something is wrong.

Being a woman is beautiful, every part of us. Knowing that having a period is the gateway to creating life, there should be no shame or embarrassment but joy and pride knowing that we women are essential to keep the world growing.

Let's Talk About It

- Does this chapter bring up a topic that you would like to discuss?
- How can you relate to this chapter?
- Does it trigger a memory?
- What is the memory?
- What emotions surfaced while reading this chapter?
- Why do you think these emotions came to surface?

_____

_____

_____

_____

_____

_____

_____

_____

_____

_____

_____

_____

...Boys

How Do I Get Him to Like Me?

Who doesn't want to feel and be loved? As a teenage girl, love is one of those topics that is in front of the mind. It is nothing like the feeling of being wanted, being the apple of someone's eye, and being claimed by someone that you are completely smitten over. I navigated my teenage years without having that feeling of someone pursuing me. There was no one openly confessing their love for me. I did not want to be left out and wanted someone to like me, so I made them. I chased boys; they did not chase me. I did not learn that guys were the pursuers, and I was the pursued. There is always some confusion about the topic of being pursued.

Being a child and hearing the older generation talking amongst themselves about how they don't approach men and the man pays for everything on dates. Then the memory of playing with the neighborhood kids and getting caught being too giddy around a boy, and out of nowhere you hear your mom or grandma saying, "you better not be chasing behind no little boy." It was an unspoken rule that we girls are not supposed to "run after a boy." This generation of women and girls are more forward and bold with going after what they want, and there is nothing wrong with that. I was the forward one. I would take it a little further and say I was flat out aggressive, and from my experience, that did not pan out too well.

New Year 5-3-2000

I really feel like s***. I have no best friend like I want and I keep going back and forth with Stanky BYRON. He dissess me cos nobody is around me. When others are around I feel like s***. I wonder if his stanky ass friend TODD has something to do with this. I like them other guys (Ashley Rippy). I really think I suck. I need to get over Byron. Just let him come some and stop worrying myself. Nussie doesn't have a clue what I feel like right now.

To my knowledge I just hope one day I stop doing something stupid like because I always lose Byron without me. I am really bummed. I just don't know what to do. I need help very badly. I U can see this was a BAD DAY!! Better luck tomorrow.

5-4-00

Today was a boring day. I didn't see Byron. I really like him but he's so mean. I have no friends either. No one ever calls me. I wish Samantha would so we can go to the movies. The Klumps is what we are going to see if we even go!! I want revenge on Byron sooooo bad. But I know God has something for him. I hope he comes to the real world and apologize to me. But who knows! He's funny acting. I want to be so pretty and cool so boys will beg for me back like (Byron). It really hurts that nobody ever calls me. I wish...

Today was a really good day. Early this morning around 1 am I got really really sick. I thought I was going to die. I didn't go to church either. My mom and Leo are going crazy because I talk hanging ugly shelf. I just hope him and Smoke don't mess things up with Byron. I hope things get better between us. Well I'm about to go.

Peace Out!!

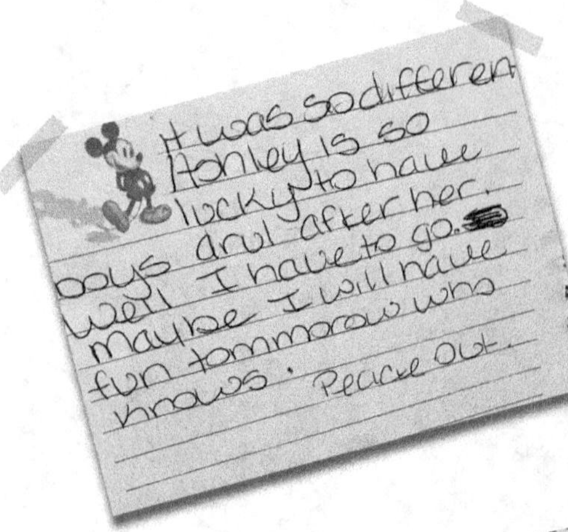

It was so different. Ashley is so lucky to have boys drul after her. Well, I have to go. Maybe I will have fun tommorow who knows. Peace out.

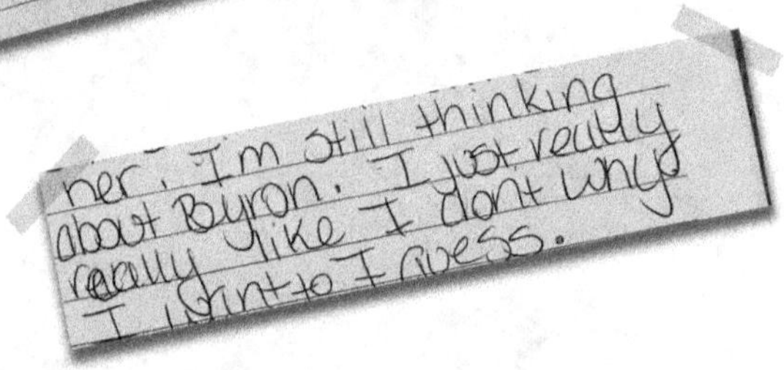

her. I'm still thinking about Byron. I just really really like I dont why I dont to I guess.

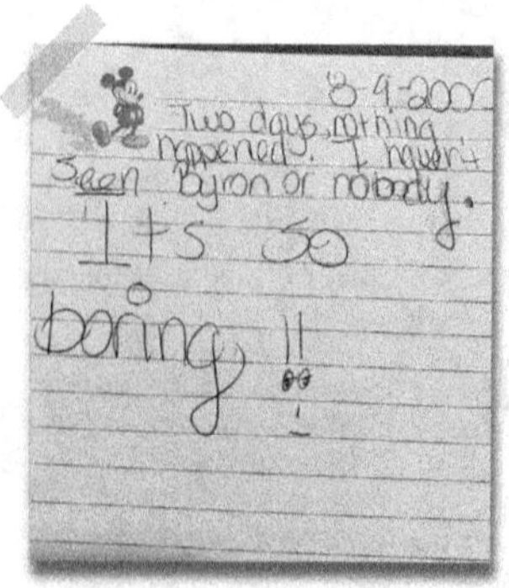

8-9-2000
Two days nothing happened. I haven't seen Byron or nobody.
It's so boring!!

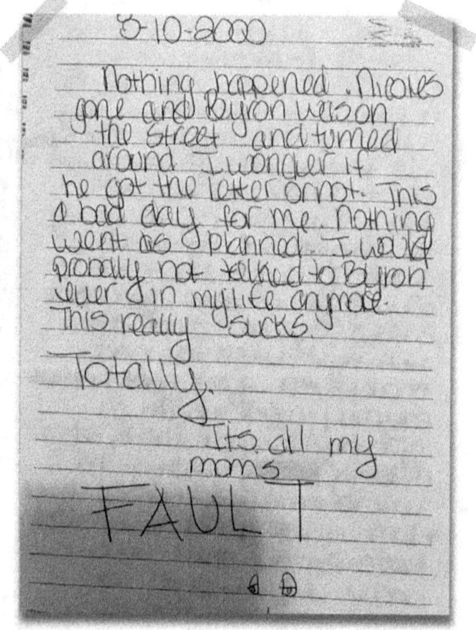

8-10-2000
Nothing happened. Nicole's gone and Byron was on the Street and turned around. I wonder if he got the letter or not. This a bad day for me. Nothing went as planned. I would probally not talked to Byron ever in my life anymore. This really sucks.
Totally.
Its all my moms
FAULT

Over the years, I heard several friends, ladies that grew up with their fathers in the home, say they are a prize. I can assume that this affirmation was planted into their self-esteem since childhood. I missed the memo, and therefore I did not know what it felt like for a guy to come at me correct, with genuine interest. Instead, I made the boys my prize.

Here is a girl that had a crush that turned into a low-key obsession. How was it an obsession, one may ask? It is easily deduced through the words my middle school heart expressed on the paper. First, the guy knew I had a crush because I made sure to tell him, my friends told him, and I'm quite sure I told him maybe three more times during our brief interactions. I should have moved along with my life after his feelings were not reciprocated, but instead, I convinced myself and others that he was just shy, and he secretly liked me. I came to this conclusion because he talked to me on the phone once. After that conversation, I applied pressure.

I would make it a point to ride my bike every day around his house. I started to hang with a friend more often that stayed closer to him, you know, to have an excuse as to why I was on his side of the neighborhood. He was going to open up to me and become my boyfriend. My delusions, not reality. How could he not? I was showing him my undying love for him. He will see my efforts, and then I will get the man of my dreams. I was just baffled why it took so long. I would call and he would never come to the phone. I would ride my bike on his street until I saw his mom's soccer van, hoping that he would see me and want to come to play. It never happened.

I became impatient and decided it was time to go a little further. I sent him a letter because he clearly was not seeing me hanging around his street. I mailed the letter. I bought a stamp and put the letter in the neighborhood USPS box! One thing about me, I have always been persistent. Trying to win this boy over to have a pre-teen puppy love experience turned into a full-blown obsession. I would wait at my living room window, hoping I see him riding his bike. I hoped and dreamed that one day he would ring my doorbell, ask me to ride bikes, or even better, ask me to be his girlfriend. That never happened.

Back in the day, us children partied. We had our own little club—music, punch, cookies, and the lights out. The club was the Dare Dance. It was the spot where you would hang with your friends, find your significant other, go kiss in the corner, pop (twerk), and come back to do it the next weekend. At the time, I only had one female friend but spent most of my weekends with my male cousin, who was more like my brother. The majority of the time, I would go to the Dare Dances with him and his crew. One particular Saturday night, my bestie was able to go, and my crush so happened to be there as well.

My girl and I put the mission in play. I positioned myself to be noticed. I knew this was my time to have my magical moment as we slowed danced to O-Town's "All or Nothing". I saw the picture clearly in my mind. He would ask me to dance and then guide me to one of the corners for our make-out session. When he saw me, he laughed. I did not take the laugh personally. I just thought he was in a good mood. To my surprise, when I finally approached him, he went in. I can't remember all that he said, but he expressed his disdain thoroughly for me. I was crushed. I felt like my heart was pulled out of my chest. I was embarrassed. The worse part was, we were around other people. I am not a girl that cries, but I cried that day. Of course, not in front of people, but I had my moment of silence for love lost.

Although this was my first blow and bout of rejection, I did not move differently with my approach to the opposite sex. It almost felt like a game to me; catch a boy, hold the boy down, wear him out, until he finally confesses his love for me, I win. When I liked a boy, I became pretty intense. I had no fear when approaching them, calling them, finding out their bus number, and even finding out where they lived. If I liked them, everyone knew, as I would have my friends speak on my behalf if they saw the boy more than I did. I am not sure what they were saying to my crush, but I trusted they were applying pressure as well, even if the guy was not interested.

Looking back, they were friends that either wanted to protect my feelings, or an enemy that wanted to see me fall apart when these guys rejected me. Either way, no one told me to chill, knowing that these boys were just not into me. Some of them were nice to me though; they would answer the phone, and we would have a good conversation, whatever would be considered a good convo to a pre-teen. However, one crush created a running joke, calling me pitiful every time he saw me. To add insult to injury, he ended up in a relationship with a friend of mine. Pitiful is a name he called me up to High School, but I carried that word in my head, my thoughts about myself. I was pitiful, I felt pitiful, and not to mention desperate.

For some reason, I did not associate my feelings of rejection with the importance of letting the guy come to me. It did not click that this would show me their genuine interest, and I did not have to be aggressive or what others will call obnoxious. In my twisted mind, and the minds of so many girls, to get the guy you want, you have to seek them out. It will give me the love I needed, and a sense of accomplishment - an ego boost. It would prove that I was worthy of love, like all my peers.

Finally, at the age of 33, I accepted the reality that regardless of how much you do or give, no matter how good of a person you are, everyone won't see you in the way you want them to, and that is okay. Not realizing this notion early in life, I created rejection in my life and diminished my confidence. Due to the lack of patience, the love void, I put myself in the position to receive constant no's and embarrassment because I did not see myself as the prize and made the apples of my eye – boys - the award. Don't get me wrong, boys and men are prizes, special, needed, and loved. At the commencement of dating, both parties should have a mutual interest. It makes for a better relationship and an even better friendship.

Please note that everyone is not as upfront with saying no as the boys mentioned above, but some guys will take advantage of a girl's eagerness. They pretend to like you with no intention of really being with you. They want the perks of you, the boost of self-esteem you give when you do and provide them with everything. This is very damaging to girl's self-esteem in the long run.

When a person's self-esteem is not in check, losing self-identity is sure to be an issue. No one realizes that the lack of self-esteem makes an individual more likely to take on the personalities of others and not embrace their own inherent individuality. Stepping into the desire to be liked and loved and trying to fulfill the desire can lead to a change in your personality to fit into other people's world, especially in the teenage years. With society dictating so much of how adolescents see themselves, how to obtain friendships, and how to maintain relationships, it is hard for a young lady to be completely comfortable with being who she is. Constant validation is necessary to feel confident and self-assured.

When trying to impress the opposite sex, I did things that I would not normally do, but I wanted to be liked so badly and to be chosen. I did not learn the concept of setting the standard and boundaries with males. Instead, I indirectly let them define me and my actions. Even worse, I perceived myself negatively because, ultimately, I was not too fond of all the things I was doing to gain their attention. It led to a toxic mindset and a vicious cycle of self-hate that took years to break.

Before thinking about dating or even building friendships, being secure in who you are will develop and maintain lasting interactions. You will not be defined by anyone else's perceptions. You are the standard; they will either have to respect it or leave.

Let's Talk About It

- Does this chapter bring up a topic that you would like to discuss?
- How can you relate to this chapter?
- Does it trigger a memory?
- What is the memory?
- What emotions surfaced while reading this chapter?
- Why do you think these emotions came to surface?

_____
_____
_____
_____
_____
_____
_____
_____
_____
_____

What's Affection?

"I love you" is just a three-word phrase, but why does it feel like a tongue twister when saying it? It could just be me that gets a lump in my throat when it comes to saying, "I love you too." I rarely heard the phrase in my household. It is not that I didn't feel love, but those words were not the norm in my family. I can recall my mom telling me she loved me the day she left me during my freshman year at Alabama A&M University, but no other times ring a bell. Since it was not common practice, it made it hard for me to be affectionate with others.

I am so uncomfortable with the concept of hugging. I never really thought about the word love and showing affection until adulthood when my little sister would come in for a hug, and I would hit her with a quick stiff hand. A hug, kiss on the forehead, or people saying "love you" was not necessary for me to know that I was loved. As people would say today, physical touch and words of affirmation are not my love language. I automatically knew my family loved me without question. They took care of me and bought me things. That was good enough, or so I thought.

As far as my other half, my dad's family, I did not think they loved me. I did not have intuitive feelings of comfort. They weren't in my life, and a phone conversation here and there ending with *I love you* did not seem genuine. I never believed them. Did this affect me? Absolutely. With them not being there for me or showing me their love, especially my father, I was incomplete. Unbeknownst to me, but subconsciously, I needed their love. I longed for it. But because there was no relationship and no trust, I sought to receive this love from other places. I had to make the people outside of my immediate family show me that they loved me.

These outside people just so happened to be boys. The only way this was going to happen was to show them first. I took it upon myself to go for the gusto, and started telling boys I loved them. What did I know at my young age about loving someone? I figured if I said, "I love you", and gave hugs and kisses, a boy would love me more than my dad ever did, and I wouldn't have to worry about his lack of attention and presence. I refer to this as misplaced feelings of affection.

At times it is hard for me to fathom and accept that for 30-31 years of my life, I believed giving outside of my emotional capacity would provide me love, in return. Saying things and pleasant formalities to others, even when I did not mean it, would get me the love I deserved and get someone to decide to make me their girlfriend. I depleted myself by giving and saying but not receiving. One day, I believed my energy was going to be reciprocated, and someone would catch this vibe. However, it never happened. I ended up continuously putting my precious energy into people that I should have paid no attention to.

The emptiness within the soul automatically makes us act in specific ways not to feel so alone. For most, including myself, we stay on searching to find fulfillment from outside sources, especially the things we want the most, up to the point that we forget to fill ourselves with love.

I did not know what a love language was as a teenager, but receiving gifts had to be it. The pattern of showering guys with gifts began to show early in my relationships. After a year or so after my first love/puppy love broke my heart and no one showed interest in dating me, I finally came upon a boyfriend. Everything happened so quickly, which should have been a flag of caution. I had continuously poured out my heart to my best friend at the time about how badly I wanted a boyfriend and to have that High School love that she was experiencing, just like many of my other peers. One phone call, and she and her boyfriend found me someone. He called me the same night. I just knew this was fate, and I could not contain my excitement. I wish I could have told you what we talked about that night, but it didn't matter the topic, I had already liked him. Why wouldn't I? He actually called!

One day before band rehearsal, I gathered a friend and my best friend's boyfriend, and we made our way to my dream guy's home. Oh, I must mention this dream guy was my best friend's boyfriend's cousin, which in hindsight, I believe this hookup was a favor rather than genuine interest. I had just started driving, and in a rush to get to the guy's home, I tried to make a light, and the car literally turned on two wheels. I scared everyone in the vehicle. I laughed at it then, but thinking about it now, I had to be the worst teen driver.

I was cute that day; I had on some green khaki cargo pants that fit my hips and butt perfectly but were loose throughout the thighs and legs, a white fitted shirt, and the infamous all-white, crisp, Air Force Ones. I like to think I made a great impression. When we got to his home, I was utterly smitten. A little shy at first, but after him showing interest in me, I loosened up. He was attractive in my eyes; dark-skinned, twist, a grill in his mouth, a white tee, and Girbaud jeans. You had to be a teen in the early 2000's urban era to understand the significance of this description. He was perfect in my eyes, and after seeing him that one time, he became my boyfriend. I can't say that this was true love, but I sure pretended it was because I finally had a boyfriend.

I would go to his house often, after school, after work. He stayed 2 minutes from my job at the time, T.J. Maxx. I took him to work when he got his first job. I also pulled up when I got word that he was planning to have a girl from his High School come over on a half-day. Of course, when I showed up, he denied the allegations. I believe that his friends stalled as he got her out of the house. I didn't really care. I was not letting go of this relationship. I wanted and needed to have a boyfriend. I let all the cheating allegations go on deaf ears. The drama inside me wanted to feel that I was still number one in his life and the other girls were stupid because he would not leave his main chick.

I never really cared about the other girls. I knew I was doing everything for him, and he would not leave me. Especially when it came to holidays and his birthday, I showed out. With my $5.25 an hour salary, I made sure to get him all the name brand attire. Good thing I worked at a place that had this stuff on discount, plus my 10% discount. I basically spoiled the guy.

One holiday stands out to me. It was our first and last Valentine's Day. The day of love had to be special. I wanted this gift to be better than the last two gifts: his birthday and Christmas. I decided to step away from the ole faithful T.J. Maxx and go to the mall where everything was full price.

After being in the mall for hours, going back and forth from store to store, and $100 later, I finally decided on a black and grey Enyce sweater. It was so expensive due to the word Enyce being leather or pleather.

Nonetheless, it was the most I've ever spent on a shirt, ever. I was proud of my purchase, and I knew this was the ultimate way to show my "love" to him. Valentine's Day comes, and he was supposed to plan the date. I was to pick him up after work, and we were going out to eat at the particular place he picked. For some reason, I felt uneasy during the day. In addition to it being Valentine's Day, it was Jordan Day. The black, white, and varsity Retro 12's dropped. We planned to both buy the Jordan's and dress alike in black and white for our date.

After waking up at 5 in the morning and standing in line for 2 hours, I was unable to get the shoe in my size. They sold out fast. I was upset and disappointed. I called him to see if he got his pair, but he did not answer. He actually did not answer most of my calls that day. When I finally talked to him, he told me he did get the shoe, but I had noticed that he did not mention him picking up a gift for me in the conversation.

I let it go, thinking he was going to surprise me with a grand gesture. I hyped myself up, and after what felt like a forced interaction between us all day, I pick him up for our date. I gifted him the sweater and card pouring out my soul. In return, I got a dollar card that reflected friendship rather than a romantic relationship and maybe a small box of candy, also from the dollar store. Our efforts did not match. Even though I was crushed, I still wanted to make the best of the love day. We ended up at Applebee's with his friend. It wasn't the best situation, and I did not feel the love.

On top of coming down with a cold that night, my stomach was in knots. I knew that the love or how I showed love did not matter, and he did not feel the same as I did. I later found out that he gave the $100 sweater away to his best friend. The nerve and disrespect! I can't tell you how much longer we were a "couple" after that night, but I can tell you that he was not around for my birthday, which was in April.

He started calling me every Thursday, only Thursdays. He was gifted his mother's car shortly after that Valentine's Day. He had planned to pick me up one Sunday. It was going to be a date where he was going to do all the treating. I waited at the window for hours, and he never called or showed. He ghosted me. No words, no *it's over*. He just moved on with his life as if I was not significant. No matter how I showed my affection, saying I love you, wanting to be around him all of the time, and buying extravagant gifts, it did not make him love or even want to be in my presence.

I am sure that not hearing I love you from my family as a common practice and not having the attention and affection from my dad's side of the family led me to overcompensate in giving my energy and gifting undeserving people. A common display of affection can go a long way, making children feel safe and secure. It builds trust and takes the need for validation from outside sources. Rewriting the non-affections is more challenging than saying I love you as an everyday practice. Proclaim your love, show your love, give your love. Make it easy for your child to see what healthy affection looks like.

Let's Talk About It

- Does this chapter bring up a topic that you would like to discuss?
- How can you relate to this chapter?
- Does it trigger a memory?
- What is the memory?
- What emotions surfaced while reading this chapter?
- Why do you think these emotions came to surface?

_____

_____

_____

_____

_____

_____

_____

_____

_____

_____

_____

_____

Why Am I Not Good Enough?

No one likes to be broken up with or ghosted, but I always seemed to get the ax by boys. It could be that I came on too strong. Ok, at times, I definitely came on too strong. In my defense, I was oblivious to what I was doing. I was going after what I wanted. But the energy that I put out there was not returned from a genuine place. This pattern was seen in all my relationships. I liked the person way more than I should have, and he either stayed because he did not know how to say that he wasn't feeling me or saw it as an opportunity to take advantage of my eagerness and kindness. I never learned from the interaction of my first boyfriend, my first love.

I approached him by expressing my interest through a note, "Do you like me? Circle yes or no." When he said yes, I pounced on the opportunity and made him my boyfriend. I was in the 8th grade and thought this was it. We would be together forever. We would be the it couple going into High School, especially since he would be the quarterback on the Freshman football team. In the midst of all of our I love yous and lovey doveyness, one day, he suddenly broke up with me for no reason. I was distraught, but not for long. I had a vision of us being together for a long time. Therefore, I set forward a mission to get him back.

Going into freshman year, we flirted with one another, but he soon got another girlfriend. I did not know how to feel. When he broke up with me, he stated that a girlfriend is not what he wanted, but yet he had one. I was jaded and upset, but I was going to work my way back to him. Long story short, we got back together, but it was only for a spell. He broke up with me again with no explanation. I saw him flirting with other girls. Why wasn't I good enough? I would ask this question often, but it was not until college where I believed that I wasn't.

I can still hear one of my good friends tell me, "Buddy said that he would never be with someone that looked like you." It took a minute for me to process what he had told me, but I immediately felt like the ugliest, most disgusting girl in the world when it registered in my brain.

Was it my weight? My skin? My eyes? I had always thought my larger-than-life eyes were the least attractive thing about me. When I heard those words, I automatically felt defeated because my confidence had started to fade from other incidents I encountered during my college experience. At the age of 33, I would love the body I had in college now, but society told me that I was fat, disgusting, and not good enough, and it told the guys that I dealt with the same thing.

The relationship between this guy and me started off as friends, but I had other plans for him. It was the accent and hazel eyes for me. Which I found out later that his eyes were contacts - the deceit! As we grew close, we spent so much time together. I would spend hours talking to him in my car. I would help him succeed in his classes. We went places, and it was fun most of the time. Then there were times when he played me, and I would have to pull up. I snuck into his dorm to confront him when other girls were there, letting my anger completely take over. I would hit him with a 1, 2. He would ask me why I was wildin', and then we would talk it out and go back to normal. This was our pattern.

This guy loved me; he said it. When we were on holiday breaks, we would continue to talk constantly. All his close friends from his hometown knew who I was, and he even called me his girl in front of them. We were basically together. Who needed the title anyway? We had grown to know each other so well in my freshman year. I knew when we got back to school for our sophomore year, he would be my boyfriend. That did not happen.

Upon returning to campus, he treated me differently. He told me that he needed his space. I did not understand. While he was home, I was his girl, but now he did not want to be around me. I wasn't going to let that happen. I stayed around. Who cared what he said. He did not hesitate to have our late-night rendezvous, or use my car for a week when I went home for my grandfather's funeral. I later heard that he was going to see other girls in my car. I still held on to him. I knew he would go back to being the person who I so desperately wanted to be with.

I gave him a little space by starting to hang with my friends more often. At this time in my life, I did not let my feelings hinder my social life, but that would all change. One particular evening after eating dinner out with my crew, we pulled up to our dorm, and this guy, my guy, was pulling out of our dorm parking lot with a girl in the passenger seat. I immediately saw red.

Three things. When he returned to school after Thanksgiving Break with a car, he became even more distant with me. Secondly, since getting his car, he did not take me out once, after all the times I took him out, drove him around, and let him use my car. Lastly, he was picking up a girl, a girl that stayed in my dorm! With all of those thoughts and feelings rushing through my body, I hit a U-turn and followed him. My friends were still in the car, and I didn't hear anything. I had tunnel vision. I was full out angry.

I finally caught up to him, and when he saw me, it was as if he saw a ghost. He sped off, and so did I. I was on his tail for a while. I had no clue what I was going to do when I caught up to him, but I just wanted someone else to feel my hurt in the moment of my rage. After a few seconds, I lost him, but I did not let it go. I drove to every restaurant on University, a main street in Huntsville, AL. After not seeing his car at any of them, I decided to wait for him at his dorm. I did not care how long that could have been. I felt justified in my anger and hurt at the time.

While waiting with my friends and his roommates, I got an epiphany. He was at the movies. I gathered my friends, we got in the car, and we were off. We pulled up to the movie theater, and sure enough, his car was there. We waited for him. As soon as I saw him and the girl exit the movie theatre, I had my friend block him in. I got out of the car and hit him with the 1 and 2, dragged him around the parking lot, and knocked his earring out. I did not feel better, but I wanted him to feel something. I followed him back to the dorm to drop the girl off, so we could talk; the same pattern we followed after he wronged me.

We talked, but I was not trying to hear what he had to say. He did not want me and he made it clear, but I was in denial. I gave him things, helped him. He called me his girl once. Why was he acting like this? I was going to make him see me as girlfriend material. I was good enough, wasn't I? I couldn't let go. I wasn't ready to feel the rejection and face the fact that I wouldn't be anyone's love interest once again.

Even after being sat down by a friend that gave me all the tea on this guy, it was hard to let go. Apparently, he had a girlfriend back home, and he was messing with this girl here and there at school. It was a punch to the gut. But I was attached to him and still wanted to be a part of his world. I did stop speaking to him, but my mind was on him. What hurt the most was that shortly after our demise, he got a girlfriend, and she and I were cool. Her appearance confirmed what my friend confessed to me, "he said he would never date someone that looked like you."

I was heartbroken. This situation affected me more than any other failed relationship. What was left of my self-esteem and confidence shattered. Moving forward, I had anxiety when it came to dating, and it continuously raised the question, "why am I not good enough?"

I had given my power and my soul to another person, and they had abused it. I associated my worth with others' thoughts or what I assumed others thought of me—a negative perception.

By the time I entered my first adult relationship, I was in a broken, fragile state. I was not a whole individual but a woman searching for a person to show me that I was good enough. I would get back in the cycle of giving, giving, and giving to feel validated and loved. I would also become a stranger to myself, trying to please and fit into everyone's world, completely losing myself. Had I learned early on to accept who I was, learned to feel that I was important, and not associate my feelings of abandonment and rejection with my worth, most of the situations I found myself in would not have affected me as much. I would have had healthier friendships, interactions, and relationships.

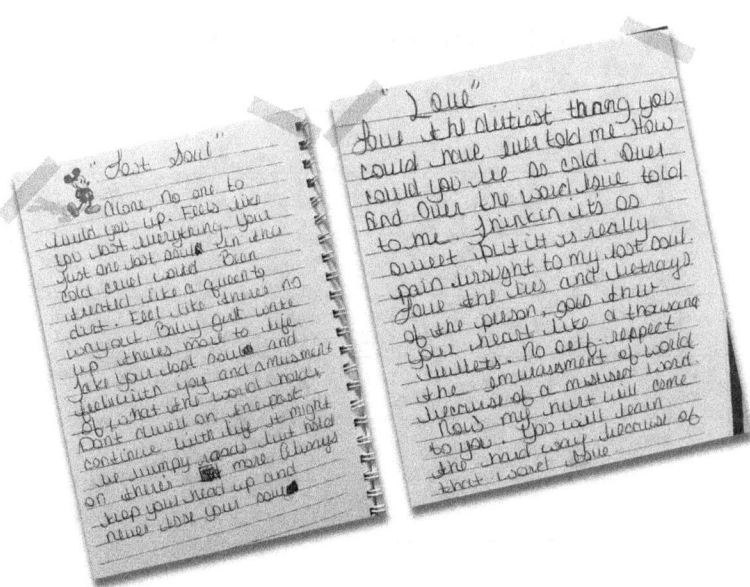

Let's Talk About It

- Does this chapter bring up a topic that you would like to discuss?
- How can you relate to this chapter?
- Does it trigger a memory?
- What is the memory?
- What emotions surfaced while reading this chapter?
- Why do you think these emotions came to surface?

_____

_____

_____

_____

_____

_____

_____

_____

_____

_____

_____

...The Talk

Should I Know About This?

From what I can remember, boys were always the center of my universe. I was very advanced at the age I should have been innocently playing with my barbies and imaginary friends. Sex was introduced to me at an early age. It was not by extreme circumstances such as rape or molestation, but by what was told by a friend who was told by a friend. Oh yea, and Cinemax after Dark. The concept of doing the "nasty" had been in my mind since before the age of 6. Was it curiosity, real attraction, longing for attention, gaining closeness to another individual, or trying to fill a void? I will say it was all the above, but way too early for me to explore.

As a kid, I had a butt; a big butt, an adult butt. Not sure where it came from, seeing as my mom, grandma, and aunts were/are petite women. Maybe it was one of many inherited features from my dad's side of the family. Regardless, my rump was intriguing to some of the boys but uncomfortable for me. It was my greatest asset and my worst enemy.

I longed for male attention because of daddy issues. Because of this, I started receiving, and I accepted the wrong type of admiration. From the many booty rubs and slaps, I felt seen and wanted. The admiration went even further. At the age of 8, my third-grade boyfriend said to me on our daily afterschool call, "I want to &#%! you." The excitement I felt was out of this world but looking back now, very disturbing. It didn't make it any better that my older sister and friend encouraged my excitement.

What do I say back? "I want to &#%! you too." Disclaimer, I am a hopeless romantic. Even at 8, I associated this phrase as an act of love and not what it really was; lust. With my declaration that I was ready to take this elementary relationship to the next level, we planned to "do it" at the bottom of the hill during recess. I eventually learned that my agreeance made me a sex symbol, objectified at the age of 8. I thought I was grown, and my 8-year-old boyfriend loved me, and we were going to "do it".

I am happy to say that it never happened. Thank the Lord! The concept didn't even make much sense. Were we supposed to lay on the grass, hide behind the bushes? Would classmates be playing kickball 50ft away? More importantly, did we even know how to "do it"? None of it made sense to me besides the feeling of being wanted. Although I did not go through with it, I did let him continue to touch my butt. Several boys did. At times they thought they were entitled to touch me whenever they wanted. I can admit this now: no matter how incredibly uncomfortable I felt, it was how I got attention, so I went with it.

The crazy thing is that the agreement to meet this guy at the bottom of the hill haunted me later in high school. My third-grade childhood boyfriend lied, which most boys do to feel like the "man". He told his friends that it happened, and in their immature minds, they believed him. He was cappin'.

One day sitting in my English 3 class, a guy tells me about the time Lil Bob (that's what we will call him for the sake of privacy) and I went down the hill. He retold an entire story, giving me details on something that I did. It caught me off guard, and even though it was nearly ten years prior, and I knew the truth, I felt ashamed and embarrassed. If he told this guy, a person who was not even a student at my elementary school, how many others did he tell? Out of all those people, what did they think of me?

I write all this to say, agreeing to something that you know is not right and dishonors who you are can follow you throughout the years. At the age of 8, I was negatively influenced, and a name was placed on me, a perception. More importantly, the perception I created for myself, I get attention through sex, stuck with me throughout most of my life.

At a young age, so many girls, primarily African American girls, are overly sexualized. It becomes their identity. Especially young black girls; we fill out more with hips, breasts, and butts earlier than our counterparts. Automatically being too fast, wearing a particular outfit that other girls of different races wear is inappropriate. Girls must not be identified by their outer appearance, but by their personality and characteristics. Learning who they are helps them make sound decisions, understand what is mentally healthy, and not disrespect themselves and their reputation.

Let's Talk About It

- Does this chapter bring up a topic that you would like to discuss?
- How can you relate to this chapter?
- Does it trigger a memory?
- What is the memory?
- What emotions surfaced while reading this chapter?
- Why do you think these emotions came to surface?

_____

_____

_____

_____

_____

_____

_____

_____

_____

_____

Why Should I Wait?

I always admired my college roommate. She was so smart, determined, and at a young age, she knew who she was and had a plan set up for her future. At the age of 17, she had it going on. More importantly, upon entering college, she was a virgin. A virgin?! She had boyfriends and love interests, and yet and still at the age of 21, graduating from college, she was still a virgin. Although, for me, having sex was a rite of passage to adulthood, I can say I wish I had taken control of my life, as my dear roommate did. I wished that I could go back and reclaim my body, my temple, and wasted time.

By the time I graduated, I was too far gone with bouts of celibacy here and there. I had good intentions of waiting for the one, but sex had become more of what was expected of me and not a real desire. As I previously said, sex was something I always knew about and had been on my mind since a very young age. By the time I got to High School, sex was the thing to do. Walking down the halls and seeing classmates pregnant became the norm. I never wanted to have a baby while in High School, but I did want to partake in the same activities as my peers. I took matters into my own hands. I planned my first time, to the T.

The male singing group, IMX (formerly known as Immature), had me ready and prepared to embark on this journey. Their song "First Time" romanticized the loss of virginity. I had to have that experience too. I pictured my first time being simply beautiful. Hopeful that the guy and I would become closer and ultimately back together because, after sex, a relationship would be a given.

Just like Mike and Alicia in the movie *The Wood*. Mike had always crushed on Alicia. They went through the years of middle school up until their Junior year, never dating. They even had significant others when they got caught up in the moment and ended up having sex. All the feelings came to the forefront, and they ended up a couple. I was excited that this would happen to me. It just had to.

I started listening to music about sex. I grew up at a time where going to the internet for information was not a thing. Music, movies, and the new era of reality TV was our learning tool. R. Kelly's (before we found out how much of a monster he was) "Greatest Sex" set the fantasy that my first time would be magical. I was wrong.

My best friend and I planned the entire ordeal. I set the exact date, time, and place. My plan did not just involve the guy and me. Mind you, I had not discussed the losing virginity plan with him at all. I knew he would agree. What 14-year-old guy wouldn't? This elaborate and calculated plan involved my best friend and the driver. The driver, who just so happened to be secretly in love with me, was supposed to pick up the guy, bring him to me, leave and go hang out at my best friend's home until we were done. It all worked out perfectly. I was so nervous; one because the thought of getting caught weighed heavy on me, and two, I was about to lose my virginity! I envisioned myself setting a romantic mood, but because of nerves that slipped my mind. Instead of having music playing in the background, the television was on, on Nickelodeon at that. Rocket Power will always hold a memory in my mind. Along with my age, this was another sign that I had no business engaging in such an intimate, mature act.

The whole thing was a disaster in a short amount of time. It brought about so much pain and no fulfillment, and to top it off, I bled for days. Afterward, I felt that my lady parts were damaged.

That first time at the young age of 15 opened a new world for me, one that I know I was not mentally and emotionally prepared for. For some reason, I felt I gained a new responsibility. I was different. I can't say if it was a good different or a bad different. I wonder if my mom ever noticed that I had a new walk. I don't believe she did. My sexual activity was never discussed.

One Valentine's Day, she found a note between a classmate and me, discussing our plans for V-Day. In the written conversation, I wrote that I was planning on getting "some", meaning I would be having sex. She did not say anything, but her mood changed from what it was previously that day. She was acting weird. Finally, before I left, she told me she did not want me to go on my date because she knew what I was planning to do.

At first, I was confused, but then she mentioned she had found my note. I became angry because, for her to see it, she did some snooping. I went on my date, and I did not have sex. The date was pretty much a disaster, and I could not bear to hurt my mom. I refrained. After that night, the note or my plan was never talked about again. It wasn't until a mild pregnancy scare that my mother had evidence that I was having sex. I did not have my period for months, and these hips of mine began to spread. My mom noticed and made me take a pregnancy test, which came back negative. She still scheduled me for a doctor's appointment. The doctor ordered a blood test. She stated that some pregnancy tests could not detect some cases, something to do with hormones or something along those lines. That was all my mother needed to hear to get confirmation that I was indeed having intercourse. She did not really talk to me for a week or two. When she came back around, we never discussed it. Life moved on. By the time I got to college, her only advice was, "you know what you need to do." Her saying, make sure you use condoms and take birth control.

After that fallout with my mom, and now discovering an irregular period, I started taking birth control, but I took a hiatus from having sex. That was until after I graduated High School. It was on and popping. For some reason, I felt that I was an adult, and I was now ready to really do adult things. I tried to hold on to the notion that this is my body, and I am in control, but I lost control as time went on. I will choose when and who I would give my essence to, but the issue was that the guys I decided on were not my boyfriends, and were not even close to any commitment. Anyone can do the physical act, but what comes after the act - the mental aspect - is what most can't handle.

What does having sex before you're ready do to a girl that really only wants love? It sends her on a mission to find love, and for me, I thought I was sure to gain it by giving my body to the guys I wanted romantically. I did not understand at the time that this way of thinking and acting on it would cause so much unnecessary trauma.

Laying down, getting absolutely no pleasure, and feeling empty after every encounter, chipped away my self-esteem. I ultimately used myself by knowingly letting men use me. There were times I knew that the situations I got into was not okay, but the hope in me, the quest for love, held the thought hostage in my head that one day someone would love what I do for them sexually, and then they would have no choice but to love all of me. I never told myself that this path was not working, and I was worth so much more than giving my precious treasure away, basically for free. I did not have much self-esteem. I felt that sex was all I had to offer.

My worth was linked to what my body provided men. Sex became my identity. If I hung out with a guy most of the time, they would expect something in return. I did not sleep with every guy I encountered, but still, I slept with enough men to internally damage my soul and self-perception. There were times I found myself in situations that I had no control over. One time, I was dragged down the hallway of a friend's apartment because their roommate demanded we have sex. He got tired of begging and decided to take matters into his own hands.

Thank God, my friend came home just as he was forcing me through the hallway. As the door opened, he immediately let me go and returned to his room as if nothing happened. My soul was crushed. This person had once been very close to me; I can't say friends at this time, but I still thought I could trust him. He was the first person I called when I found myself in an even more disturbing situation in the school year before.

After hanging out with this guy and having a few drinks, I fell asleep, only to wake up with the guy having sex with me. There was no permission given. I didn't want it, yet he felt that he could have his way with me as I slept. I froze and did not know what to do. When tears started to fall from my eyes, he did not stop. I guess he thought my tears were because I felt pleasure. When I finally came to, I told him to stop and to get up. I left and never talked to him again. Trauma. What made the situation even worse, my friends said that I wanted to have sex because I went over to his home. Trauma. My trust in people diminished after those two incidents.

I declared that I would be in control and never put myself in a situation where someone else would hurt me. The issue is when you don't deal with the hurt from traumatic events, taking control of your life seldom works out with a positive outcome. I got to the point of calling whoever I wanted in my space whenever I wanted it and moved along as if nothing happened. It felt liberating at times, but these actions did not protect me. I would come upon another situation in adulthood that reflected my first rape. This time, because I thought I had the situation under control, I continued the act, hoping to dominate him. It didn't work. I felt depleted, sad, and ashamed.

I wanted to be respected and enjoyed in other ways outside of giving away my body, but I did not know how to articulate my wants properly. I knew the guys that I was involved with did not care about me. How could they? I did not care about myself. I had become so numb to being used by men. I blocked out any emotion that would be associated with hurt and sadness and continued the situationships with the undeserving. These men ultimately had control over me and my actions. This made it hard for me to feel, to trust, and to set boundaries.

The lesson in all this is that your body is your own, and no one is entitled to it. Ever! Regardless of your situation with the person, if sex is not what you want, the decision is already made. If they don't respect your boundaries and decision the first time, then they are not the boy or man for you. Repeatedly asking you for sex or making you feel guilty enough that you engage in the act is a form of rape.

Your choice is good enough. The emotional damage resulting from doing things you are not ready for creates dangerous cycles. A little piece of your power, and a small part of your glow diminishes when you make decisions based on others' expectations of you rather than your expectations for yourself.

Let's Talk About It

- Does this chapter bring up a topic that you would like to discuss?
- How can you relate to this chapter?
- Does it trigger a memory?
- What is the memory?
- What emotions surfaced while reading this chapter?
- Why do you think these emotions came to surface?

_____

_____

_____

_____

_____

_____

_____

_____

_____

_____

_____

Conclusion

How to Keep the Conversation Going?

I want to thank you for taking the time to read a small fraction of my life. I never thought I would be here expressing my vulnerability for the world to see. It was and is necessary. There is a freedom with being able to express yourself and have the right people listen. It is a great comfort knowing someone is there with you through all of your woes in life. I found myself not being able to have that freedom or comfort growing up. I had lost trust in people at a very early age and expressing myself became harder and harder as I grew older. My disconnection from the adults in my life left me no choice but to internalize all my unpleasant feelings and make misguided decisions on my own. I was mentally and emotionally broken the majority of my life. I am now at the point of complete healing, bettering myself every day, and finally forgiving those who hurt me but, more importantly, forgiving myself.

Let's Talk About...Boys is the conversation starter for women and girls to sit down and learn from one another. My story is shared to influence women to heal from their past and share their truths with the young ladies in their lives. My purpose is to help build a foundation and a safe space for girls to have open and honest dialogue without fear but with confidence in knowing they have the support of the women closes to them.

To continue in keeping the conversation going, turn to the next page for Let's Talk About...Boys Discussion Guide. It is time for generational cycles to be broken. It starts with you!

With Love,

Londen Chanell Underwood

Discussion Guide

...The Men

In the chapter, "Why Doesn't He Want Me?" Londen describes her feelings of rejection and abandonment from her father. Often, young girls who have absent fathers go through these emotions, and often they cannot express their feelings, but it does come out in their actions and behaviors. They chase what they are missing. In the case of an absent father, they go after boys. In this guided discussion, be open to changing the narrative of a healthy family dynamic, not using others to feel the void, or what it feels like to be rejected in any aspect of life.

Ladies to Girls

What is your definition of rejection?

Has there been a time, or are you currently struggling with feelings of rejection? Tell me more about these feelings.

What do you feel that you needed from me or others in the past?

What do you feel that you need from me or others now?

Do you find yourself needing more attention than your peers?

Do you feel that you get the proper attention from me, your father, siblings, stepparent, or other relatives?

Is there something in the past that has hurt you or changed your view of a family member? Tell me about the situation.

Girls to Ladies

Did you feel rejected or abandoned in your childhood?

How was it growing up in a single-parent household?

How was it growing up in a two-parent household?

What did you learn from your parents?

Did you feel like anything was missing when you were my age?

Did you feel that you acted out to fill a void when you were my age?

How did your childhood have an impact on how you raise me or interact with me?

In "Why Can't I Be (Walking on Eggshells)," Londen explains how she got to a place of uncomfortableness, in a place that is supposed to be most secure, her home. Often, adults automatically assume that their children will adjust to their characteristics, feelings, and thoughts and will grow up to be just fine. In reality, some behaviors and parenting styles should be changed and not passed down from generation to generation. A child not being able to be themselves in the home or afraid of the extreme consequences makes them withdraw, rebel, or resent their parents. Anger management is something we laugh at but is something we should take more seriously. Anger is often mirrored and passed on. How we react to certain situations can make a whole world of difference and impact. The questions below will help explore the safety within the home and how interactions can improve to make everyone comfortable with being themselves.

Ladies to Girls

Do you feel that I yell at you?

How does it make you feel?

Is there anything within the household that makes you feel like you have to walk on eggshells or makes you uncomfortable?

How would you suggest we handle conflict within the home?

How would you feel safe and comfortable at home?

Do you feel protected?

Is there anything in the home that you don't like how it is handled by your father, siblings, stepparent, me, or other relatives?

Are there things you are holding on to from the past that we haven't dealt with?

Girls to Ladies

Are there things or discipline styles you view as normal because of your childhood experiences?

How was the discipline in your household?

Did you fear your parent's reactions?

Did you feel comfortable in your home?

Do you react to me in this way because it was done to you?

We have all dealt with loss, whether it be a death or ended friendships and romantic relationships. All of these situations need to be appropriately grieved. When things hurt, we try to bury the feelings instead of feeling them, causing suppression until explosion. That explosion looks differently based on the individual. Some examples include anger, depression, or anxiety. Facing our feelings of loss can alleviate some pain and make every day a little more manageable every day.

Both

Is there something you worry about?

What situation brings anxiety into your life?

Are there times you feel withdrawn or lonely?

Is there a situation you are grieving?

Are there things you would like to discuss with a professional?

How do you feel that _____ is no longer here or around?

...My Body

Body issues are something we all face. Society sets the standard. The Society Fairy told us what is acceptable and what is not. Differences are rarely accepted, making most of us always worried about what we look like to others rather than how we feel about ourselves. This pressure causes insecurities and low self-esteem in most cases. The insecurities we hold on to can be transferred to the people in our lives without knowing it. Being confident in yourself and your looks influences your daughters to be satisfied with themselves. Acceptance is also vital when it comes to helping build the confidence of the younger generation. Being accepted is an essential component of building self-esteem in every aspect of life.

Both

Do you feel confident in yourself?

What don't you like about your body?

Ladies to Girls

Do your peers make you feel that you need to change the way you look?

Do you feel attractive?

How do you maintain your confidence?

What are somethings you would like to do together to create healthier lives?

Are there some things I say that make you feel self-conscious?

If you have feelings of imperfection, what would be something you would want to hear from your loved ones?

Talking about the changes going into womanhood can be a taboo conversation. It is something all girls go through, but most girls have not had the proper discussion to understand and accept the changes they are going through. Entering the beginning stages of womanhood is one of the most important experiences teen girls will go through and should be celebrated and treated as such.

Ladies to Girls

Have you talked about your menstrual cycle?

Are you uncomfortable or ashamed while on your menstrual cycle?

Is there something that you don't understand?

Have you noticed symptoms during your time of the month?

What would you like to know before it happens?

Girls to Ladies

Did you talk about your menstrual cycle when you were growing up?

What did the talk consist of?

Who was involved in the conversation?

Did you find it helpful?

...**Boys**

Girls tend to have feelings for boys first. It can contribute to the science that girls mature faster than boys. In those cases, if the boys are not feeling girls simultaneously, it can cause some feelings of rejection on the girl's part. It is essential that girls understand that their feelings are acknowledged and let them know it is okay for boys to choose not to be interested in them. Having the option to choose gives the freedom to explore one's wants. It does not have to be a devastating thing if someone does reciprocate the same feelings. Young ladies should be reassured that they have an opportunity to find someone genuinely interested in them rather than wasting their time and energy on someone that does not care for them. Equal interest and time create healthier relationships.

Ladies to Girls

Do you have any crushes at the moment?

Do you have a significant other?

Do you find yourself nervous around the opposite sex?

Do you find yourself seeking attention and doing things you

wouldn't normally do?

What is considered a healthy relationship?

What does it mean to be too forward?

Girls to Ladies

What was dating like when you were my age?

How did you know a guy liked you?

Did you experience puppy love?

Were you able to have a boyfriend while in school?

Did you have to sneak to talk to your crushes?

In "What's Affection?", Londen expresses that she longed for love from her father's side, therefore making her seek love in other places. She even tried to buy other's love. Londen learned a hard lesson that affection has to be a two-way street, or you would end up giving with no appreciation or receiving.

Ladies to Girls

Have you found yourself going over beyond and not receiving anything in return?

Why do you feel like you did this?

How did it make you feel?

Why is it important for someone to have a mutual interest in you?

What are other ways to show your interest besides gifting or having sex?

When is it okay to decline a gift?

In what ways can you give yourself affection?

Girls to Ladies

Have you given too much in your relationships?

How did it make you feel?

How did you learn to balance?

What steps do you feel you should take to change the narrative of a one-sided relationship?

In the chapter "Why Am I Not Good Enough?", Londen feels close to entering a relationship but was hit with the reality that the person she wanted did not want her back. Her looks were at the forefront of the guy's decision not to pursue a romantic relationship. She questioned her worth tremendously after this relationship. It took a lot of rebuilding to get to the point of truly accepting herself and knowing her worth. Having self-worth and self-awareness early in life gives a layer of protection when faced with rejection or objectification.

Ladies to Girls

Has anyone ever made you feel less of a person and unworthy?

What is your definition of self-worth?

How can other's views and thoughts of you have power over your life?

Why is it important to believe one's actions rather than words?

What do you need to learn and understand about accepting someone's no?

Girls to Ladies

Has a guy ever made you feel unworthy?

How did you move past it?

Did you lose your sense of self in a relationship?

What are somethings you would recommend to build self-worth after a toxic relationship?

...The Talk

Sex is such a hard conversation to have, especially with younger generations. The topic is well known but rarely discussed in a healthy manner. Children often learn about sex from outside sources other than the home. Young ladies having a conversation with an adult can provide more insight into making the decision not to engage in the act or the proper precautions after making the decision. That talk can also provide insight into the emotional and mental aspects of engaging in sex. Make the conversation more comfortable by being truthful, realistic, and understanding.

Ladies to Girls

What do you know about sex?

What questions do you have about sex?

Have you thought about having sex?

Have you had sex?

Do you feel pressure from your peers to have sex?

If you are having sex, are you practicing safe sex?

How do you feel now after having sex?

Are you still with the person you lost your virginity with? Were you in a relationship when it happened?

Are you familiar with the different types of sexually transmitted diseases?

Do you know what is considered rape and sexual harassment?

What representation are you setting for yourself?

Have you done things that affected your self-respect?

Does social media bring pressure to do certain things or be a certain way sexually?

Girls to Ladies

Did you talk about sex with your mom before engaging in it?

Did you feel pressured by your peers to have sex?

How did you feel after losing your virginity?

Did your relationship last after engaging in sex?

Were you in a relationship when you lost your virginity?

Have you ever been in any uncomfortable situations?

Do you have any regrets?

What is something that you wish you knew before engaging in sex?

Your Thoughts

Your Thoughts

Your Thoughts

Your Thoughts

Your Thoughts

www.ingramcontent.com/pod-product-compliance
Lightning Source LLC
Chambersburg PA
CBHW051406290426
44108CB00015B/2176